Americans Move West

Rosie McCormick

Core Knowledge

ISBN: 978-1-68380-472-7

Americans Move West

Table of Contents

Going West by Land and by River

When the first European settlers came to America, they thought the whole country was unsettled land—a frontier. Of course, Native Americans lived on this land, and had done so for hundreds of years!

Later, settlers built towns and cities along the East Coast. After settling much of the East Coast, people began to move west to find more land. And so the frontier itself moved west.

People moved west a little bit at a time. One problem to overcome was the fact that the Appalachian Mountains stood in the way. Daniel Boone realized this when he first followed Native American trails over these mountains to reach the land beyond.

So Daniel, with help from others, made a trail for settlers to travel on. The trail was called the Wilderness Road. Many settlers followed in Daniel's footsteps. They moved west into Kentucky and other areas where Native Americans already lived.

Settlers moved west in different ways. Some hiked along the trails made by men like Daniel Boone. Others traveled on horses or in wagons pulled by oxen or mules. Still others followed rivers.

On the western side of the Appalachian Mountains, there were some rivers that ran west. Many people floated down these rivers on flatboats. A flatboat is a boat built out of logs. Some flatboats had cabins. Families would put everything they owned—clothes, furniture, even animals—on board.

Flatboats could go in only one direction—downstream, the way the water was flowing. They had no motors and no sails, so they had no power. Slowly, though, people began to use a different kind of boat, called a keelboat.

Keelboats had sails to drive them along. Keelboats could float downstream *and* go upstream. Getting upstream wasn't easy. If there was a strong wind, the sails *might* provide enough power. Usually,

though, boatmen had to stick long poles into the river and push with all their might.

Going West by Steamboat and Canal

By 1800, the steam engine had been invented. The steam engine burned wood or coal to heat water that then turned into steam. Robert Fulton knew that the steam engine could be used to power a certain kind of boat— a steamboat. A steam engine would turn large wheels and give his boat the power it needed to go upstream. Robert Fulton set out to build a steamboat.

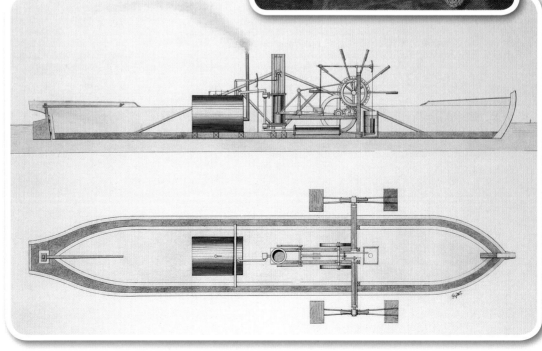

In 1807, he finished the steamboat and named it *Clermont*. The *Clermont* was almost 150 feet long. It had a cabin where passengers could sit, and rooms where they could sleep.

Fulton steamed up the Hudson River from New York City to Albany, a distance of 150 miles. It took sailing ships four days to make this journey. Fulton's *Clermont* could complete the trip in only a day and a half.

Robert Fulton wanted to work on another project that would also help Americans move west—the building of the Erie Canal. A canal connects two bodies of water. The Erie Canal connects Lake Erie, one of the five Great Lakes, to the Hudson River in New York State. The governor of New York, a man named DeWitt Clinton, agreed to build the canal.

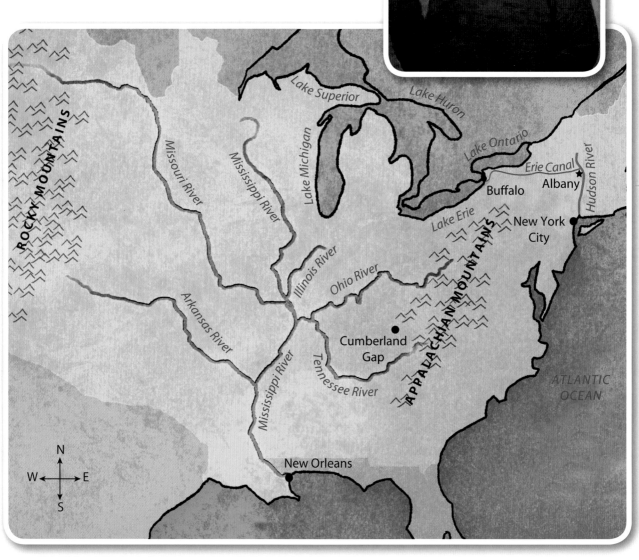

Digging the Erie Canal was a big job. Thousands of people worked on it for several years. The canal was more than three hundred miles long. The workers also built eighty-three sets of canal locks.

A lock is a part of the canal that moves boats up or down by raising or lowering the water level in the lock.

In 1825, the first canal boat made its way from Buffalo, on Lake Erie, to New York City. It carried a barrel of lake water from Lake Erie. Governor Clinton dumped the water into the Atlantic Ocean to show that these bodies of water were now connected.

The Erie Canal made it possible for more people to go west and for farmers out west to send their crops east, to New York City. Other goods could be sent by canal to New York City too. New York City grew quickly, thanks in part to the Erie Canal.

The Oregon Trail

American settlers crossed the Appalachian Mountains and began to settle in the Midwest. They traveled on the rivers, and they used the Erie Canal to get there. They crossed the Mississippi River and explored the Great Plains. But as they moved farther west, something else was in their way—the Rocky Mountains.

The first settlers to explore the western mountains were called mountain men. These men were fur traders. They traded with Native Americans who had lived in this mountain area for hundreds of years.

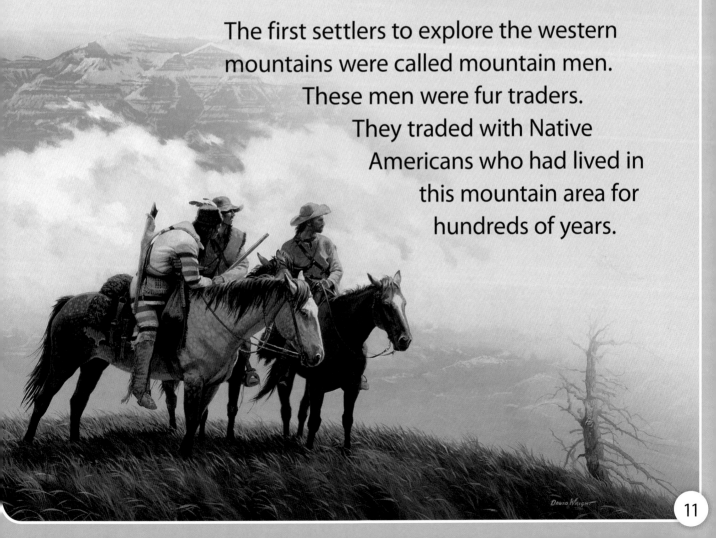

Jedediah Smith was a mountain man. He was a hunter, trapper, and explorer. There are tales of him fighting a bear single-handedly. Jedediah and others explored a route through the Rocky Mountains, called South Pass.

After Jedediah made it through the Rocky Mountains, others followed. Eventually, settlers reached the Pacific Coast and the areas known today as Oregon, Washington, and California.

People often moved west in wagon trains. It took them almost six months of traveling every day to reach the Pacific Coast. Most people walked the entire way. The trail they traveled on earned the name the

Oregon Trail. The trail ran from Independence, Missouri, to Oregon.

Wagon trains always left Independence, Missouri, in the spring, when the cold weather was over and the snow had melted. People would gather outside town and wait until there were enough travelers to make a wagon train. When they were ready, they would set off, a line of wagons winding across the land.

It was also important to wait for the grass to grow. The oxen and mules that pulled the wagons needed grass to eat. If the wagon train left too early in the spring, the animals would not have enough food or water.

People needed lots of supplies too. A family of four needed enough food to make it to Oregon. The people in wagon trains took lots of flour and bacon with them.

People also piled all their belongings on the wagons—furniture, clothing, pots and pans, and farming tools. That's why most people walked. The wagons were just too full!

Sometimes, people packed more than their animals could pull. Then they would have to get rid of things. Often, travelers left items along the side of the trail, and people following behind picked them up.

The California Gold Rush

When James Marshall looked into the river, his eyes nearly popped out of his head. There, just beneath the water, at the edge of the river, was a shining rock. Marshall picked up the rock. It was a piece of gold!

James was helping to build a sawmill in California. The year was 1848. California was now part of the United States. James and his boss, John Sutter, knew they had found gold. They tried to keep the discovery a secret. But it didn't stay a secret for very long.

Without cell phones and computers, news about the gold did travel slowly. But eventually the news reached the eastern part of the United States. Over the next three to four years, thousands of people, hoping to get rich, moved to California. Some went to start businesses; others went to mine for gold!

People called the miners "forty-niners" because so many of them came to California in 1849. As well as Americans, thousands of people traveled across the Pacific Ocean to search for gold. Many came from China.

One way to search for gold was to "pan" for it. Using a pan, a miner would scoop up gravel from a stream. Then the miner would hold the pan under the water for a few minutes. The flowing water would wash away all the gravel and leave the heavier gold flakes behind.

A man named Levi Strauss traveled to California with a strong denim fabric. Levi Strauss hoped to make tents out of the strong fabric and become rich. But other people had gotten there first. Miners already had tents. So Levi looked around and noticed that miners' pants were full of holes from mining or panning for gold.

Most miners wore pants made out of soft cotton fabric. Levi Strauss used his fabric to make strong denim pants. Thousands of miners bought Levi's pants. People like Levi, who started businesses, often became richer than those searching for gold.

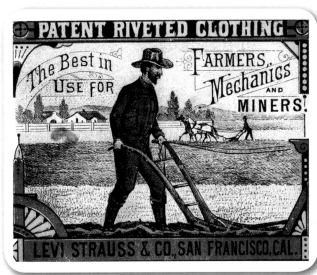

The Pony Express

In 1860, two businessmen were looking for horse riders who were daring and brave. The two men were starting a mail delivery business, called the Pony Express. At the time, it took months for mail to be delivered across the United States. These two businessmen set out to change that.

The Pony Express was a horse-and-rider relay system. The Pony Express started in St. Joseph, Missouri, and went all the way to Sacramento, California. Mail could also be brought from the East to St. Joseph and then be taken to the West. The Pony Express promised to deliver the mail in only ten days.

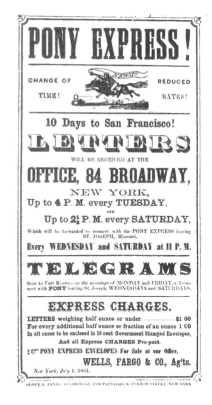

Here's how the Pony Express worked. Relay stations were set up on the route about every fifteen miles. Each station kept fast horses. Riders got a fresh horse at each station and rode on as fast as they could.

Most Pony Express riders were teenage boys. The youngest was eleven years old. His name was Bronco Charlie. One day Charlie was at the Pony Express station when a horse came in without his rider. Charlie rode the horse to the next station in record time, so he became a regular rider.

The Pony Express lasted only a year and a half. A new kind of communication called the telegraph replaced it. The telegraph could send and receive messages using wires and signals. When the Pony Express started, the telegraph lines only went as far as Missouri. But soon after, the telegraph lines reached all the way to California. There was no longer a need for the Pony Express.

The Arrival of the Railroad

The first American railroads in the United States were built in the East to connect big cities. Building a railroad was hard work. Railroad tracks had to be laid down. This hard work took many strong men.

Then, during the 1860s, two American railroad companies decided to build the transcontinental railroad. The Union Pacific Railroad started at Omaha, Nebraska, and laid tracks going west. The Central Pacific Railroad started in Sacramento, California, and headed east. When this new railroad was finished, it would carry people and goods from place to place in about a week.

Both companies needed thousands of workers to build the transcontinental railroad. The Central Pacific company brought in many Chinese immigrants to work on the railroad. The Union Pacific company hired many Irish and German immigrants to help build its part of the railroad.

The transcontinental railroad was completed in 1869. To celebrate, the two companies met at Promontory Point, Utah. The workers from the two companies shook hands. Then a golden spike was driven into the ground. Thanks to the "Iron Horse," it was now possible to travel all the way from New York to California by train.

Life out West

Many people who moved west kept cattle on ranches. A ranch is a large farm, but instead of growing crops, ranchers raise cattle. Texas was a big ranching area. People set up ranches that went on for miles and miles. Cowboys guarded the cattle. They also trained wild horses.

Cowboys trained wild horses in a fenced area called a corral. A wild horse was led into a corral to have its first saddle put on. Then a brave cowboy would jump on the horse.

Untrained horses were called bucking broncos because they would buck and jump. They were not used to having someone on their back, and they didn't like it.

In the spring, cowboys went on a long trip. Back East, people wanted to eat western beef. So cowboys drove the cattle north from Texas to Kansas and Missouri, where the railroads then transported the cattle.

A group of cowboys would drive as many as two thousand cattle almost one thousand miles across open land to a railroad town.

The Trail of Tears and the Death of the Bison

As settlers moved across America, they met many different Native American groups who had lived in various places for a very long time. The American government was now taking more and more Native American land and giving it to settlers. Native Americans were being squeezed onto smaller areas of land and pushed farther west.

When Andrew Jackson became president, he ordered the Cherokee to leave their land in North Carolina, South Carolina, Tennessee, and Georgia. Andrew Jackson sent soldiers to force them to march to new land in Oklahoma, more than eight hundred miles away.

The Cherokee were forced to march many miles without resting. Many people died along the way. This was a terrible act of cruelty. The Cherokee called their journey the Trail of Tears.

The incoming farmers and the new railroads that ran across parts of the Great Plains threatened Native American people. This was especially true for the Sioux and the Comanche, who had made the Great Plains their home.

The Great Plains were also home to the American bison. The bison were very important to the Native Americans who lived on the Great Plains. The Native Americans hunted the bison for food.

They used bison hides to make clothing and tepees. Bison bones were used to make tools. Native Americans even used parts of the bison as fuel for their fires.

Native Americans watched as wagons and the railroads brought thousands of settlers onto the Great Plains. The settlers planted crops, raised cattle, started businesses, and built towns. They did all of this on Native American land.

Other Native Americans came to the Great Plains too, having been forced off their own land somewhere else. They too had to find ways to survive in their new home.

One thing that Native Americans did to survive was to sell bison hides to the settlers. The hide was valuable because it could be turned into leather. So, bison were hunted for their hides.

Sadly, Americans also hunted bison for fun! They shot large numbers of bison for sport while aboard moving trains. Bison numbers became smaller and smaller. Without the bison, the Native Americans of the Great Plains could not survive.

The move west hurt Native Americans of the Great Plains and beyond in many ways. They lost their homelands and their way of life. Many died in clashes with settlers, or in battles with the U.S. Army. Some Native American leaders did try to accept the changes that were happening.

Others, such as Crazy Horse and Sitting Bull, fought back against American settlers and U.S. soldiers. They won some battles, including the famous battle at Little Bighorn.

Crazy Horse

Sitting Bull

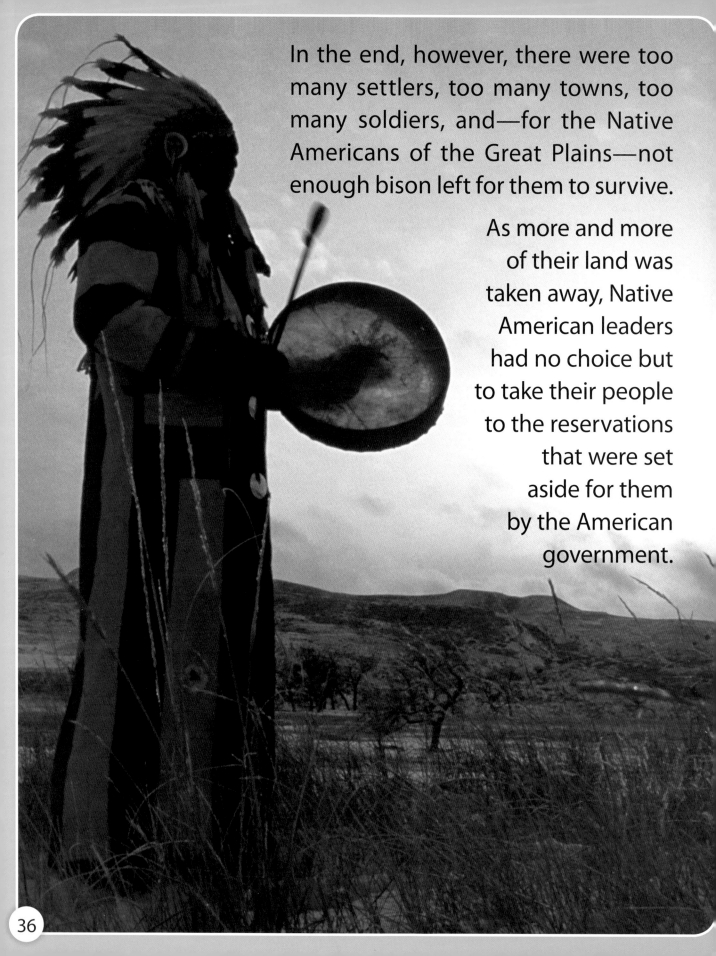

In the end, however, there were too many settlers, too many towns, too many soldiers, and—for the Native Americans of the Great Plains—not enough bison left for them to survive.

As more and more of their land was taken away, Native American leaders had no choice but to take their people to the reservations that were set aside for them by the American government.

Sequoyah and the Cherokee Language

Sequoyah was a Cherokee who grew up in what is now Tennessee. Sequoyah had been a soldier in the U.S. Army. When he was a soldier, Sequoyah noticed that some people were able to communicate with one another by looking at pieces of paper.

Sequoyah called these pieces of paper "talking leaves." Later, he learned that people could communicate by writing down symbols that made words.

The Cherokee people had no written language. Sequoyah began to think how useful it would be if his own people could use "talking leaves." Sequoyah decided to create a system of reading and writing for his people.

Sequoyah worked on his system for more than ten years. His friends and family thought he had gone crazy.

Sequoyah realized that all Cherokee words were made up of sounds, or syllables. Sequoyah developed a system with eighty-five symbols. Each symbol stood for a syllable.

Cherokee Alphabet

D a	R e	T i	Ꮔ o	O u	i v
S ga Ꭷ ka	Ꮄ ge	Ᏹ gi	A go	J gu	E gv
Ꮺ ha	Ꮮ he	Ꭿ hi	Ꮶ ho	Ꮁ hu	Ꮻ hv
W la	Ꮟ te	Ꮧ ti	G lo	M tu	Ꮩ lv
Ꮳ ma	Ꮵ me	H mi	Ꮉ mo	Y mu	
Ꮎ na Ꮏ hna Ꮐ nah	Ꮑ ne	Ꮒ ni	Z no	Ꮔ nu	Ꮕ nv
Ꮖ quu	Ꮹ que	Ꮗ qui	Ꮴ quo	Ꮄ quu	Ꮛ quv
Ꮜ sa ꭲ s	Ꮄ se	Ꮁ si	Ꮿ so	Ꮞ su	Ꭱ sv
Ꮷ da Ꮝ ta	Ꮪ de Ꮫ te	Ꮧ di Ꮨ ti	Ꮩ de	Ꮪ du	Ꮫ dv
Ꮧ dla Ꮭ tla	Ꮮ tle	C tli	Ꮰ tlo	Ꮱ tlu	P tlv
Ꮳ tsa	Ꮴ tse	Ꮵ tsi	Ꮶ tso	Ꮷ tsu	Ꮸ tsv
Ꮹ wa	Ꮺ we	Ꮻ wi	Ꮼ wo	Ꮽ wu	Ꮾ wv
Ꮿ ya	Ᏸ ye	Ᏹ yi	Ᏺ yo	Ᏻ yu	Ᏼ yv

Sounds represented by vowels.

a as a in father or short as a in rival   *o as aw in law or short as o in not*
e as a in hate or short as e in met   *u as oo in feel or short as u in pull*
i as i in pique or short as i in pit   *v as u in but, nasalized.*

Consonant Sounds.

g nearly as in English, but approaching to k. d nearly as in English, but approaching to t. h, k, l, m, n, q, s, t, w, y, as in English.
Syllables beginning with g, except Ꮝ have sometimes the power of k, a. s. sᴠ are sometimes sounded to, tu, tv; and syllables written with tl,
except Ꮮ sometimes vary to dl. — Pendleton's Lithography, Boston.

Sequoyah taught his daughter, Ahyoka, to read and write using the symbols he had invented. Sequoyah decided to show the system to the Cherokee chief and his council. Sequoyah left his daughter alone with the men. Ahyoka wrote down the words the men spoke. Then Sequoyah came back and read the words out loud.

Then Sequoyah wrote words and Ahyoka read what he had written. The Cherokee leaders were very happy to see that Sequoyah had made reading and writing in the Cherokee language possible.

THE OREGON TRAIL

INDEPENDENCE

ROCKY MOUNTAINS

OREGON CITY

Transcontinental Railroad

Baltimore

Omaha

Nebraska Terr.

Promontory Point

Utah Terr.

Sacramento

San Francisco

California

42

Core Knowledge®

CKHG™
Core Knowledge HISTORY AND GEOGRAPHY™

Series Editor-in-Chief
E. D. Hirsch Jr.

Editorial Directors
Linda Bevilacqua and Rosie McCormick

Subject Matter Expert

J. Chris Arndt, PhD, Department of History, James Madison University

Illustration and Photo Credits